DINING AREAS

DINING AREAS

A PRACTICAL GUIDE TO DESIGN AND DECOR

JULIE LONDON

MEREHURST

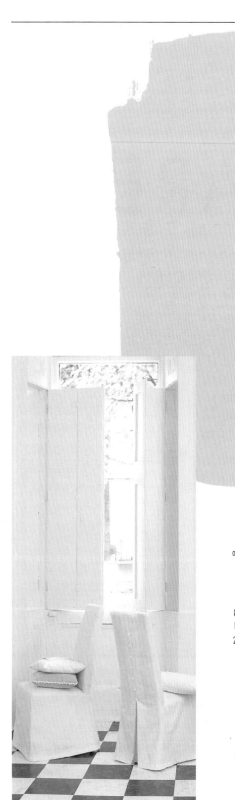

First published in 1997 by Merehurst Limited,
Ferry House, 51-57 Lacy Road, Putney, London SW15 1PR

Copyright © Merehurst Limited 1997

Hardback ISBN 1 85391 542 4
Paperback ISBN 1 85391 608 0

A catalogue record of this book is available from
the British Library

Edited by Cally Law
Designed by Sue Miller
Special photography by Tim Imrie
Styled by Clare Louise Hunt
Illustrated by Susie Morris/Brihton Illustration

Colour separation by P&W Graphics, Singapore
Printed in Italy by Olivotto

ACKNOWLEDGEMENTS

The publisher would like to thank the following photographers and
organisations for their permission to reproduce the photographs listed:

ROBERT HARDING SYNDICATION: pages 4, 7, 18 & 22 — James Merrell;
pages 8, 24 & 43 — Jan Baldwin; page 9 — Polly Wreford;
page 10 — John Heseltine; page 11 — Tim Imrie; page 12 — Simon
Page-Ritchie; pages 14, 17 & 25 — Christopher Drake; pages 16 &
23 — Lucinda Symons; page 21 — Trevor Richards; page 26 — David
Barrett; page 62 — Simon Brown

CAMERA PRESS: pages 18, 19 & 20 — Schöner Wohnen;
page 49 — Brigitte

ELIZABETH WHITING & ASSOCIATES: pages 4 & 15 — Neil Lorimer

INTERNATIONAL INTERIORS: page 1 — Genifer Witbeck; page 24 — Albert
Turrick; page 25 — Kristina Ratia

HOUSES & INTERIORS: title page — Simon Butcher

Contents

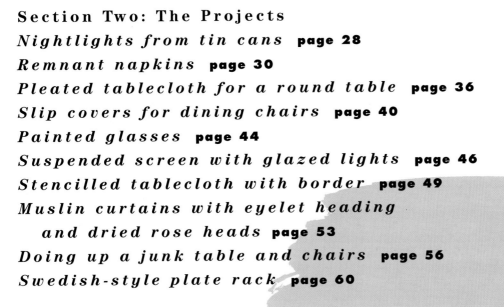

Introduction

The room in which you eat is often the hub of the house, and the table is the focal point for many activities other than eating. It obviously makes good sense for the dining room to be near the kitchen and, because you want people to linger over their food and conversation, the mood needs to be intimate and the furniture comfortable.

A separate dining room is a luxury these days, but if you do have one, make the most of it. It could be that it also doubles as an office, a playroom, a place to show off your treasures – even a greenhouse. The fact that it has to be functional at certain times doesn't mean that a dining room can't be an area of calm and tranquillity at other times.

Often the dining area is part of the kitchen or living room, which means you have to juggle the two functions of the room – furniture has to be flexible and the room must be decorated to serve two purposes. However, you can create a two-room effect with lighting and the clever positioning of furniture.

There are many things to consider when planning a dining area, but first you must decide how many people in your family sit down for meals together, how often you like to entertain, and for what other purposes the room will be needed.

A patchwork quilt makes an unusual tablecloth,
but it has inspired this colour scheme.

Chapter one

Table settings and room decoration

When it comes to decorating a dining room, the scheme will depend on several factors, such as whether it is a separate room or part of another, the existing furniture, the available light and the mood you are trying to create. Your choice of colour or theme could be inspired by your china or curtains – or maybe you need a neutral backdrop for stronger accent colours or interesting furniture. Red is a traditional colour for dining rooms and it does promote an intimate atmosphere, but it can be difficult to live with all the time and is best reserved for separate dining rooms. Whatever colour combination or theme you choose, stick to it as closely as possible – too many styles and colours can create a cluttered look and will feel claustrophobic.

Seating

It is difficult to estimate how many people you can seat around a table. For a start, it depends on how friendly they want to get, but as a rule 60 cm (24 in) per person is a good guide. If your chairs have arms, about the width of a pair of crossed arms – or 70 cm (28 in) by a depth of 35 cm (14 in) – is adequate for each place setting. Something else to bear in mind when seating people is the position of the table legs. Most of us have spent at least one uncomfortable meal with our legs straddling the table leg.

If you are trying to find chairs for a table you already own, take the height of the table with you when you go shopping. Chairs with arms should fit underneath the table for comfort and to save space. Try to allow 30 cm (12 in) between the chair seat and the tabletop.

Setting a table

Most dining is fairly casual these days and when it comes to setting a table for dinner there are no strict rules.

Set places so that guests are evenly spaced around the table, trying to give them a minimum of 60 cm (24 in) each.

Lay cutlery according to the order of eating. The first cutlery to be used should be on the outside of the setting, so that you start at the outside and work your way in. Knives (with the blade facing the plate) and spoons go on the right of each place setting; forks on the left.

Glasses stand on the right above the knives and spoons. Use a wide goblet for red wine or water, a small wine glass for white wine and a smaller version yet for sherry or liqueurs. If you are only using one glass, a stemmed goblet will suffice.

The side plate should be on the left of the place setting and to the left of the cutlery, with the napkin on top of it.

Special occasions

Decorating a table for dinner is the icing on the cake. Take time to plan what you are going to do and match it to the occasion.

Keep to a theme and follow it through to the china, cutlery, napkins and candles. Be creative: outline each place in ivy; put a fresh flower on each plate; tie up cutlery with ribbon; write out the menu and place cards on handmade paper.

Your theme could be a colour or a birthday. Try painting glasses (see page 44) either to match china or with the name or favourite thing of the birthday person. Use cotton sheeting instead of a tablecloth and dye or paint it. It is cheap enough to use for one special occasion.

A centrepiece can be matched to the occasion. Keep it simple

and effective: floating candles and flower heads in a decorative bowl of water; a small group of flowers displayed in tin cans; an arrangement of candles of different heights; a pile of presents; a bowl of fruit to be eaten for dessert. Keep the centrepiece low so that guests can talk easily to each other over the top of it.

For a children's party buy a block of sugar paper and use the sheets as table mats; cover the table with a paper tablecloth, give them crayons and let them draw; tie brightly coloured balloons to the backs of chairs and let them take them home afterwards.

Tablecloths and napkins

Unless you want it to be floor length, a tablecloth should have an all-round drop of 25–30 cm (10–12 in) so that it falls a little below lap level and your guests don't get tangled up in it. To a certain degree, a cloth will protect the table, but a felt table pad underneath allows you to put warmed plates and dishes safely on the cloth without marking the table.

Table felt is available from department stores, or look through the classified ads in home magazines for mail-order companies who will cut it to size to fit your table.

Right: A napkin is a theme on a plate — ribbon, ivy, raffia and parcel tags all make amusing and individual napkin rings.

With so many pretty paper napkins available why bother with the fabric variety? Because they provide an opportunity to dress the table and create a little theme on a plate. Be imaginative and use twisted ivy, ribbon, parcel tags, dried flower heads, raffia, beads, copper garden tags and handwritten cards. Personalize each napkin for your guests.

For birthday meals, a little present attached to the napkin with ribbon is a nice touch; at Christmas, tie baubles with curling ribbon. There are loads of things you can do...

Fabric napkins don't need to be expensive. Cut them from remnants to match colour schemes, or make each one different (see page 30). Scour the remnant bins in shops for unusual fabrics at bargain prices. Dress fabrics are ideal for making napkins as they are designed to withstand regular washing. If you use furnishing fabrics, wash them first to remove any dressing or special finish.

Chapter two

Dining areas as part of another room

Most dining areas are borrowed from another room, usually the kitchen or living room, but a dining area in a large hall or conservatory is not unusual. New houses are often built with just one room downstairs which has to double as both the living and dining area. So how do you decorate a room that has to serve more than one purpose?

Create different moods by using lighting and furniture to highlight separate areas of the room while keeping the same colour throughout. Freestanding open shelves can divide a dining area from a sitting area without blocking any light and will provide useful storage space for both rooms. Two large rugs on a wooden floor can contain dining and sitting space within their boundaries.

Another way to create a separate dining area is by using a moveable physical barrier such as a suspended screen to isolate a kitchen from its storage area (see page 46) or muslin on a curtain track (page 53). A freestanding screen will partially separate the table to give the dining area an intimate feel, and can be folded back against the wall when not in use.

The space under the stairs is often under-used, yet this alcove can make a cosy dining area in a small house. Shelved, it will also provide valuable storage space for crockery and glassware. Another often-forgotten space for eating is the hall. Some older houses and flats have enormous hallways that will easily accommodate a large dining table and chairs. Such an arrangement could create a wonderful entrance to any property.

Many people decide to build a conservatory to give themselves an extra room, but if there isn't a separate dining room this would be an ideal opportunity to create one. Conservatories are lovely to eat in and by their very nature have views over the garden and an intimate atmosphere when the sun goes down.

Above: An impromptu dining area can be set up in the corner of any room.
Right: A run of units separates the kitchen and dining areas.

14

Chapter three
Multi-purpose dining rooms

In a small house space has to work hard, so even if there is a separate dining room it can't always be totally devoted to eating and entertaining and will probably have to serve more than one purpose.

A dining room may also need to be an office, sewing room or playroom, so you must think about how you will use the room before you decide what furniture it will require.

A large dining table can double as a sewing table or, if the dining room is to be used as an office, you might prefer a smaller table to leave plenty of room for filing cabinets and a computer table. There may be a need for extra storage to cater for hobbies, or for a small desk for studying or doing household accounts.

It could be that this is the only room in the house where it is possible to get

Right: Painted fabric panels can be drawn to disguise storage when the table is used for entertaining.
Below: Hide clutter under a fitted tablecloth.

any peace and quiet – perhaps an armchair and footstool would fit in, along with a shelf for books and magazines.

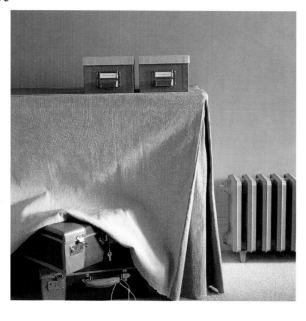

Chapter four
Lighting

Lighting is very important in a dining area. Too much light and you feel as if you are under a spotlight – too little and you can't see what's on the table.

It is difficult to light two areas in the same room for different purposes, but it can be done.

A rise-and-fall pendant will give a pool of light which can be focused on to the table, while candles combined with background lighting such as wall lights, table lamps and up-lighters will create a more intimate mood.

If your dining area is part of the kitchen the lighting may be too bright, because you need more light to prepare food than you do to eat it. One solution is to have kitchen and dining lights on separate switches, preferably dimmers, so that the kitchen lights can be turned off – or at least dimmed – when you eat. Or switch off just the main kitchen lights and leave on the under-cupboard lights.

The focal point of any dining area is the table, so intimate lighting is needed here. A rise-and-fall pendant will cast an intimate pool of light on the surface and can be removed

when the table is not in use. To prevent dazzling your guests, bulbs should not be visible from seating positions. If they are, use crown silvered bulbs.

Candles are a must for that intimate feel, but they can be a bit dim just on their own. Use candles on the table, but keep them below eye-level or you and your guests will be continually peering around them to keep conversation going.

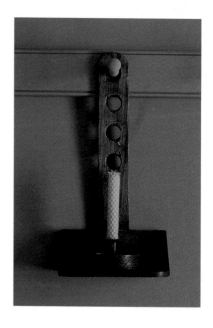

Chapter five

Flooring

Right: Woven rush matting, which can be taken out and shaken, provides warmth underfoot in this shared kitchen/dining room. Below: An inlaid border adds a defining edge to a wooden floor. You could create this effect with a stencil and paint.

Dining-room floors should be practical and hardwearing, yet comfortable underfoot. Always go for something that is easy to keep clean, but don't forget the look. A dining-room floor can be somewhere to experiment, so why not try out your painting and stencilling skills.

If your dining area is part of the kitchen, then you will have the same flooring throughout. Consider yourself lucky if you still have the original floorboards, as a wooden floor is both modern and practical. Painted and sealed with varnish, it will be easy to keep clean. Treat it as a canvas – stencil round the position of the dining table and chairs to distinguish the dining area from the kitchen area. Laminated wood and wood-effect vinyl are also simple to clean.

Linoleum is perfect for kitchen-diners as it can be cut to almost any design. To distinguish the dining area, simply take a pattern – maybe from curtains or wallpaper – and transfer it to the floor.

Quarry and terracotta tiles are fine for a country-style kitchen but they can be expensive and need a certain amount of upkeep; ceramic tiles will do the same job and are much

cheaper. The drawbacks with these types of hard floor are that they are cold underfoot and that anything dropped on them will break. A heavy object might also break the tiles.

When the living and dining areas are shared, go for something comfortable and smart that will not show the dirt too much. Again, a wooden floor is smart and practical, and a

couple of large rugs will help to define each area. Fitted carpet is also popular and if this is your choice, pick a carpet with an inbuilt stain protector. You can also have an existing carpet cleaned and then protected.

Seagrass is an alternative to carpet. Woven from natural grass fibres, it can be made into rugs or fully fitted. It creates a good transition from living to dining areas, but be careful what you spill on it as the weave can be difficult to clean.

Chapter six
Furniture

Dining rooms in small houses need adaptable furniture – extendable tables, folding chairs, sideboards and shelving for storage. And, as the dining area is so often part of the living room or kitchen, dining furniture needs to fit in with other furniture.

Right: Patio chairs can double as dining chairs and lend an informal feel to a room.
Below: Loose covers willl update favourite chairs that have seen better days.

Choose a table to suit the space available. A round table will seat more people in comfort and takes up the same floor area as a square one. A gateleg table is useful when space is in short supply – it folds down to a slim size and will sit against a wall when not in use.

An extendable table makes sense if you like to entertain but have limited space. Loose leaves mean that the extra leaf has to be kept somewhere when not in use. Integral leaves make a table heavy, but you do save the extra storage space which may be put to better use. See how the table extends and note the position of the legs in relation to where everyone sits. A central pedestal won't be in anyone's way.

Whatever you decide, the most important thing is to choose a table to suit your needs. For example, a large table in the kitchen may take up a lot of room, but it also gives you an extra work surface.

Garden furniture can also double as dining furniture and is a reasonably inexpensive way of furnishing a dining room. Garden chairs are useful for extra seating and loose covers will make them appear more substantial.

Comfortable chairs are vital, or no one will want to linger at the dinner table: seats should be deep and not cut into the backs of legs at the front edge; chair backs should give support without being too rigid. Upholstered seats and backs are the most comfortable and are best suited for a shared living room. Wipeable chairs are advisable in a kitchen/dining room, but add washable seat cushions for extra comfort.

Slip covers (page 40) or tie-on seat cushions will bring new life to old chairs. They also provide an opportunity to make a colour link with other decoration in the room.

Whatever chairs you choose, sit on them before you buy. And make sure they fit neatly under your table or they will waste a lot of space.

In a small house, furniture needs to be adaptable and storage is all-important.

China

It is convenient to store china, glass and cutlery close to the dining table. If the space is available, a sideboard with cupboards and drawers is a good idea. This will also provide a surface from which to serve food and drinks. A Swedish-style plate rack (see page 60) keeps plates to hand and is a good way of showing them off if you have a particularly decorative collection.

Open shelves are versatile and can store and display crockery successfully. Organize china and glass neatly – an arrangement of plates or bowls can be as pleasing to the eye as a favourite painting.

Basic white dinner plates will take you through any social occasion. Buy bone china as this will last a lifetime and longer, while earthenware will chip and wear relatively quickly. White china can be mixed easily with other colours and patterns. Try to keep to a colour theme – blue and white works well, and there is a lot of this colour combination around.

Choose a colour theme when starting a china collection. Blue and white are eternal and mix well with other colours.

Chapter seven
Tableware

The right china and cutlery should take you through any occasion. Choose a dinner service that you can add to. Basic white china, or a design from one of the well-known potteries, can be supplemented with bright Continental earthenware. The same goes for glassware and cutlery – choose readily available designs and build your collection at your own pace.

Car boot sales and junk shops are a good source of cheap and unusual china and glass.

If you have old pieces that you want to match up, contact the manufacturer as the design may still be in production. Or try one of the china-match services which you will find in the classified ads sections in the back of home interest magazines. Usually these specialize in just one or two manufacturers, but they are worth a try if you have fallen in love with a particular design.

Caring for china

To avoid scratching plates when they are stacked, lift them from the top, don't pull them out from the bottom. Most new china is dishwasher-proof, but if you are buying old pieces wash them by hand. Hard water deposits can be removed with diluted vinegar.

Glasses

Wine glasses should be large enough for you to swirl the wine around the bowl to release the smell and flavour, without it ending up in your lap! Tulip-shaped glasses are the best for wine, but they should be easy to drink from full or nearly empty.

On the table, have a glass for red, a glass for white and a glass for water. Serve aperitifs and liqueurs in small glasses –

you can use the same one as long as it is washed inbetween.

Store glasses in a cupboard, on their stem – they will pick up any smell in the cupboard if they are stored upside down. If the glasses have not been used for a while, wash them before they are used.

Cutlery

When buying cutlery, hold the pieces in your hand and feel how comfortable they are. Does the handle sit well in the palm of the hand? Does the weight and size feel right? Are there any sharp bits that will irritate under constant use?

Choose a design that has a full range of pieces. Start with basic knives, forks, dessert spoons and teaspoons, and add to them as you can afford to. Alternatively, mix different designs together as long as the pieces are roughly the same size and weight.

Stainless steel is the most hard-wearing material for cutlery. Look for the figures 18/10 or 18/8. These refer to the percentage of chromium and nickel (which increase resistance to stains and corrosion) added to the base metal.

Silver-plated cutlery has a thin layer of silver over a base metal and is more expensive

Above: Unusual cutlery adds the final touch to a table setting and will pull a theme together.
Right: Beautifully presented crockery can be as pleasing to the eye as a favourite picture.

than stainless steel. Most of it comes in traditional designs that are still around today, so if you inherit solid-silver or silver-plated cutlery, the chances are that you will still be able to find pieces to match.

Acrylic handled cutlery comes in many clear colours and can add sparkle to a table setting, but it is usually only available in the four basic pieces – knife, fork, spoon and teaspoon.

Project one

Nightlights from tin cans

Candles at the table always create an intimate atmosphere and make an unusual centrepiece. These nightlights are based on Shaker-style punched-tin lanterns.

1 Take the top off the can using a traditional can opener with a butterfly side handle that leaves the rim intact.

2 Cut the tracing paper to match the depth and circumference of the can. Work out the pattern on the tracing paper – keep to simple shapes that are easily identifiable, such as stars, hearts or fish.

DEPTH

CIRCUMFERENCE

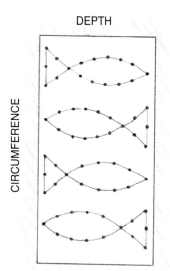

You will need

- Plain tin cans of varying sizes, used for fruit or vegetables (not soft drinks)
- Tracing paper
- Masking tape
- Drill with a metal bit
- Candles

4 Using a metal bit on your drill, drill holes where you have marked the dots. Be careful not to let the can or drill slip. The can may buckle under the pressure, but it is easily straightened.

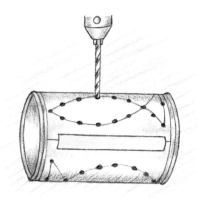

3 Mark dots at intervals along the outline of the shapes – not too close together – and tape the tracing-paper image around the outside of the can.

Project two

Remnant napkins

Napkins are the easiest thing in the world to make. If you use leftover fabrics they can match the rest of the room. Just make sure that any fabric you use is washable.

You will need

- 50 cm sq (20 in sq) cream fabric for each napkin
- 2 m (79 in) ribbon for heart napkin
- Matching thread
- Contrast fabric for heart, patchwork and appliqué napkin
- 4 m (4½ yd) ribbon for buttonhole napkin

Heart napkin

1 Cut the napkin fabric to 50 cm (20 in) square. Turn a 1.5 cm (⅝ in) hem on to the right side of the fabric and iron to keep in place.

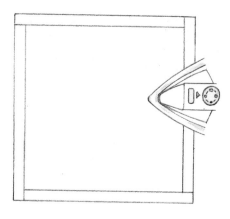

2 Cut four 50 cm (20 in) lengths of ribbon, allowing for a 1.5 cm (⅝ in) hem on each length. Pin the ribbon to each hemmed edge of the napkin, turning under the hem and overlapping the ribbon at each corner. Stitch the ribbon in place.

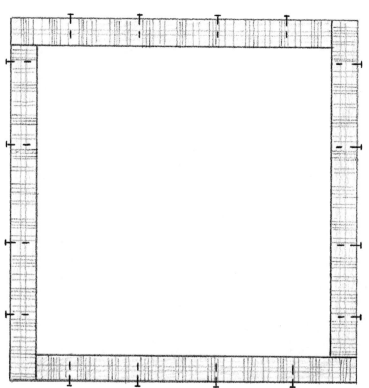

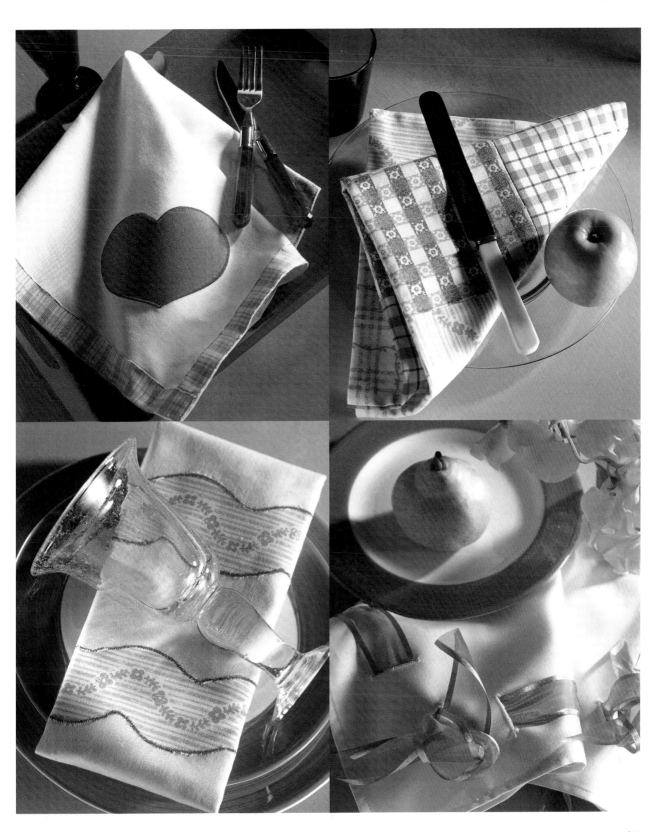

3 Trace a heart shape on to contrasting fabric. Cut it out and pin it on to the corner of the napkin. If you have a sewing machine, satin-stitch around the edge of the heart. If you are sewing by hand, use two strands of thread together for a more substantial edge.

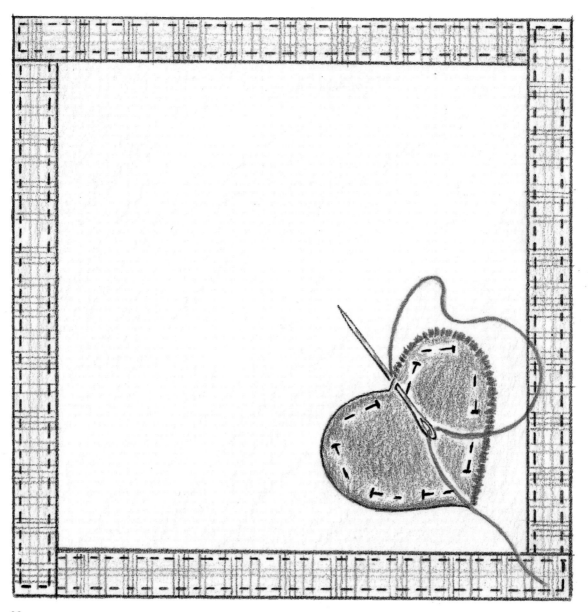

Patchwork Napkin

1 Cut four 15 cm (6 in) squares from four complementary fabrics.

2 Sew four of the squares – one of each fabric – together in a strip, with a 1 cm (½ in) hem on each seam.

3 The next three strips are sewn together in the same way but each square moves along one place horizontally.

4 The four strips are then sewn together to make a square.

5 With right sides facing, sew the square to plain fabric the same size, leaving an opening to turn the napkin right sides out. Press and sew up opening.

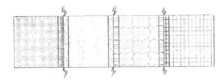

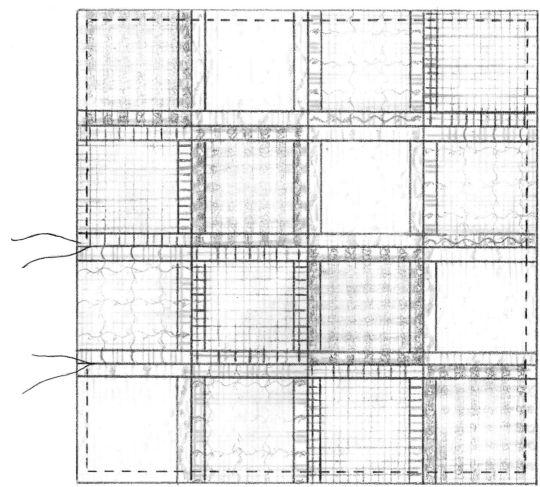

Appliqué Napkin

For this one I used a wavy flower pattern, cutting the pattern to follow the design of the fabric. You could use any fabric with a simple pattern — maybe leftover curtain fabric.

1 Cut the napkin fabric to 50 cm sq (20 in) and cut two wavy strips in contrasting fabric for the appliqué, following the printed pattern.

2 Pin the appliqué fabric to the napkin fabric, keeping the design towards the centre so that it can be seen when folded. Carefully satin stitch the appliqué in contrasting thread.

3 Turn a hem on the reverse side to hide the raw edges.

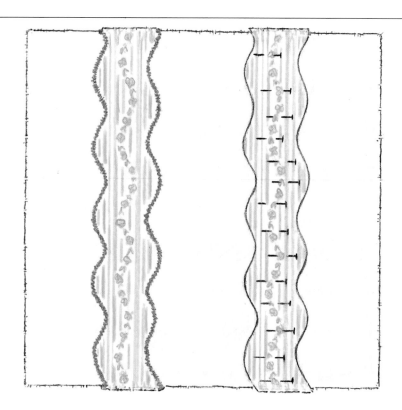

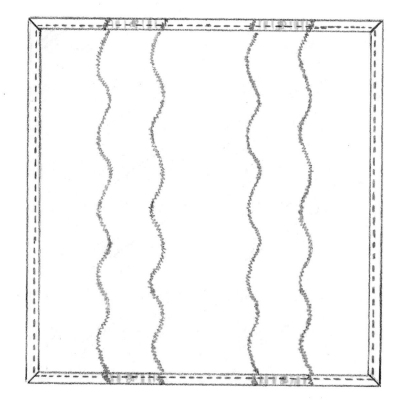

Ribbon and buttonhole napkin

1 Cut the napkin to 50 cm (20 in) sq and turn under and machine a narrow hem.

2 Mark out the position of the buttonholes with a pencil – one on each corner and four along each side of the napkin – so that the ribbon threads through the holes and ties in a knot at the corner.

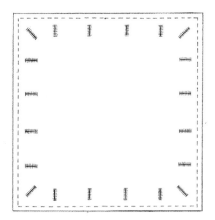

3 Sew each buttonhole by hand or by following the instructions given with your sewing machine. The length of the buttonhole will depend on the width of the ribbon you intend to use.

4 Cut four equal pieces of ribbon, at least one and a half times the length of the napkin. Thread through the buttonholes, with two ends coming out at each corner and tie in a loose knot or a bow if the ribbon is long enough.

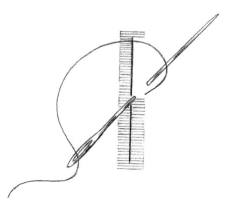

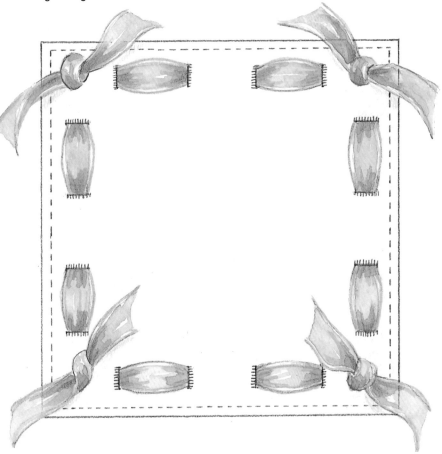

Project three

Pleated tablecloth for a round table

T ablecloths never seem to fit round tables properly. This pleated
cloth fits perfectly and uses about two metres of fabric,
depending on the size of the table. Be sure to choose contrasting
complementary fabrics for the cloth and internal pleats.

You will need

- 2 m (79 in) fabric
- 50 cm (20 in)
  contrasting fabric
- Matching thread
- Sewing machine

1 Measure the dimensions of the
table top – the one I used had a
104 cm (41 in) diameter and 320 cm
(10½ ft) circumference. The drop of
the tablecloth is to be 20 cm (8 in).

2 Cut a circular piece of fabric for
the table top, adding a 2 cm
(¾ in) hem allowance. Cut four rectangles of the same fabric, 82 cm
(32¾ in) x 22 cm (8¾ in) for the drop.

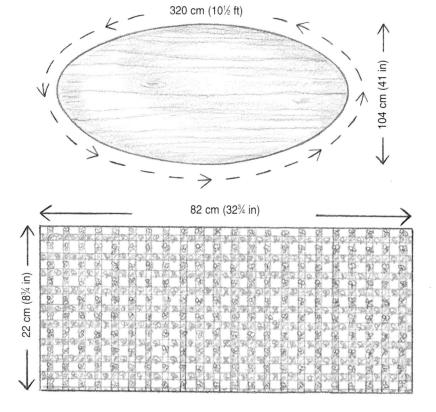

320 cm (10½ ft)

104 cm (41 in)

82 cm (32¾ in)

22 cm (8¾ in)

Also cut four 22 cm (8¾ in) squares of fabric from a contrasting fabric for the inverted pleats.

3 Join all eight pieces together alternately, giving each join a 1 cm (½ in) seam.

4 With right side facing, place a pin vertically in the centre of the contrast fabric pleat and fold the border fabric in towards the pin and then back on itself. Pin the fabric in place and repeat on the other side. Pin the other three pleats this way.

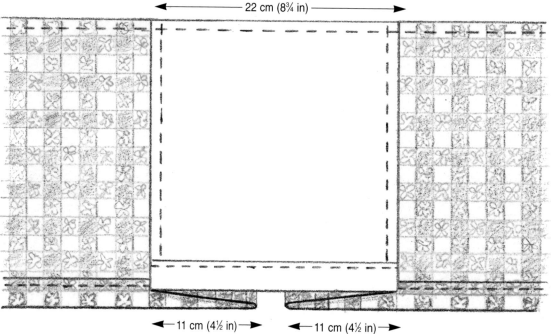

← 22 cm (8¾ in) →

← 11 cm (4½ in) →   ← 11 cm (4½ in) →

5 Pin and tack the border on to the circular top and sew in place.

6 Turn up a 1 cm (½ in) hem and press. The cloth should fit the table exactly.

Variation

1 To make the border, instead of cutting four rectangles of fabric, cut one strip, 15 cm (6 in) by the circumference of the table, plus 1 cm (½ in) seam allowance at each end.

2 Cut another strip of cream contrast fabric, 7 cm (3 in) deep by the same length.

3 With right sides together, sew them horizontally with a 1 cm (½ in) seam and press the seam open. Then join the two sides together with a 1 cm (½ in) seam. Press this seam open. Join the border to the top fabric with a 1 cm (½ in) hem.

Project four

Slip covers for dining chairs

How often do you keep furniture you don't like because it is too good to throw away? This way you can update your old dining chairs to co-ordinate with your room, or cover different chairs to give them a unified look.

You will need
- A dining chair
- Fabric
- Piping cord (buy more than you need and wash before use as it shrinks)
- Matching thread

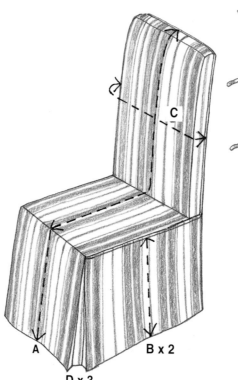

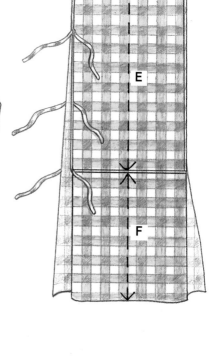

1 Measure the chair as shown and make a paper pattern for each of the nine (A, B x 2, C, D x 3, E and F) pieces. Use pattern tracing paper, available from department stores and haberdashers. Cut out all the pieces and label with a piece of paper and a pin so you know which is which.

2 To make the casing for the piping, cut 3 cm (1¼ in) strips, diagonally across the grain of the fabric. You will need enough piping to edge the sides, up and across the top and back of the seat. Join the strips right sides together, and press the seams open.

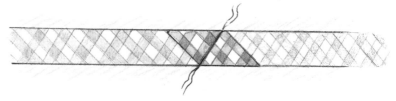

3 Cut the casing and the piping cord to the right lengths and tack the cord inside the casing.

4 With right sides together and the piping in the middle, sew the piping to the two back pieces E and F. Continue to join all the seams with piping in this way and insert the front (two) and back (one) pleats (D) as for the pleated tablecloth (see page 36). Keep trying it on the chair to make sure it fits.

5 To make the ties, cut six strips of fabric on the straight of the grain, 3 x 40 cm (1¼ x 15¾ in). Turn

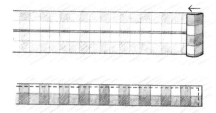

a 1 cm (½ in) hem down each side and at one end, press. Then fold the strip in half and sew along its length. Repeat on the remaining five strips.

6 To join the ties to the back, pin them to the inside back and the inside side of the chair cover, check for position and make sure each tie is level with its opposite. Sew in place by hand.

7 Put the cover on the chair and pin up the hem. Take off the chair and either machine or sew by hand.

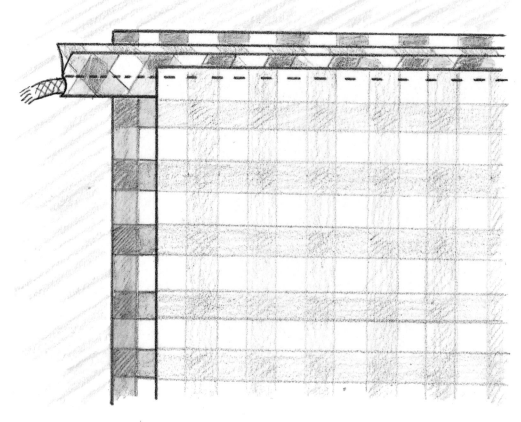

Variation: Chair with bow back

1 Make chair cover as before, but instead of ties cut out four rectangles of fabric, 100 x 20 cm (39½ x 8 in).

2 With right sides facing, sew two rectangles together, leaving an opening on one of the shorter sides and cutting off the top corner on the other short side.

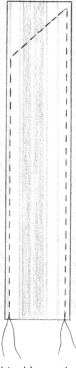

3 Repeat with the other two rectangles, cutting off the bottom right-hand corner instead.

4 Turn them right sides out and press, sew on to the back of the chair as for the ties. The right-hand bow will have to be sewn into the seam at the same time as the piping.

● **For special occasions:** If the chair underneath is in good condition, make your cover from voile or organza. You can stencil or hand-paint the cover with fabric paints and pens to personalize it.

Project five
Painted glasses

Paint glasses to match your china or decorate them for a special occasion such as a birthday or wedding. Glass paint is reasonably permanent so wash glasses by hand using a soft cloth or sponge and do not rub the design.

You will need
- Glasses
- Pearlescent glass paint
- Paintbrushes

1 Wash the glasses in hot soapy water and dry with a glass cloth. Remove any glue from price labels with methylated spirits.

2 Use one colour at a time or the paints will run into each other. To make the spots, dot blobs of paint and leave to dry.

3 Outline the spots in a different colour and leave to dry. Continue building up the layers of paint until you get the intensity of colour that you want. I gave these glasses four coats of paint.

Variation:
Cut shapes from sticky-back plastic to stick on to the glass. Trace numbers from a book to encourage children to count, or cut thin strips of different colours and stick on in a continuous spiral.

Project six

Suspended screen with glazed lights

This novel way of isolating an area of a room without closing it off completely allows the screen to be moved along the length of the room on a ceiling-mounted track. Where conventional doors would encroach on the useable space, this sliding screen offers the perfect solution in any dual-purpose room.

1 Cut the sheet of MDF to size. Mark out the position of the squares for the coloured acetate with a pencil.

2 Drill two pilot holes inside two opposite corners of the marked squares. The pilot holes need to be big enough to get the jigsaw blade in. Cut out all the squares and sand the edges.

3 Give the MDF panel a coat of acrylic primer on both sides.

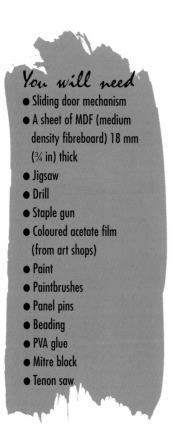

You will need
- Sliding door mechanism
- A sheet of MDF (medium density fibreboard) 18 mm (¾ in) thick
- Jigsaw
- Drill
- Staple gun
- Coloured acetate film (from art shops)
- Paint
- Paintbrushes
- Panel pins
- Beading
- PVA glue
- Mitre block
- Tenon saw

3 Give the MDF panel a coat of acrylic primer on both sides. Leave to dry. Give it two coats of eggshell paint, rubbing down lightly between coats.

4 While the paint is drying, fix the sliding track to the ceiling, following the manufacturers instructions. You may need to join two kits together. Make sure you screw the mechanism into the ceiling joists to hold the weight of the MDF.

5 When the panel is dry, attach the rollers from the sliding-door mechanism kit to the top edge of the door. When screwing into the end of MDF it is necessary to drill a small pilot hole for each screw to prevent the wood from splitting. Staple-gun the coloured acetate film to the reverse side to cover each of the square holes. Cut each piece of acetate 3 cm (1¼ in) bigger than the hole, so that there is an edge to staple on to.

6 Cover the staples with a mitred square. Cut four equal lengths of beading for each aperture. Mitre the corners using a mitre block and tenon saw and glue the corners together. When the glue is dry, tack the mitred squares over the staples holding the acetates in place.

7 Hang the panel on to the mechanism (you will need at least two people to do this) and make any necessary adjustments.

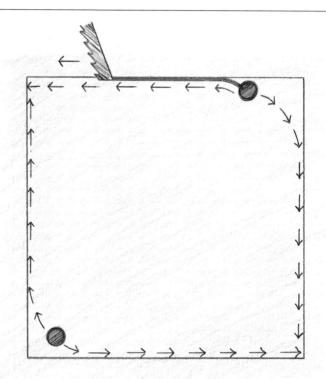

Project seven

Stencilled table cloth with border

The stencil design for this tablecloth was taken from a Sixties vase found at a car-boot sale. Use stencils to give an old tablecloth a new lease of life or make your own from scratch with cotton sheeting. Buy sheeting in king-size widths for a cheap way to cover a large table. You can use remnants to make the border.

You will need

- Cotton sheeting to make a tablecloth and four napkins
- Contrast fabric for the border
- Dylon fabric paint
- Dylon fabric marker pen
- Matching thread
- Stencil card
- Craft knife

1 Cut the sheeting to the required size for your table. Your stencilled design needs to hang well over the edge of the table.

2 Trace the design from the vase (or any other reference) on to tracing paper and transfer it to stencil card. Cut it out with a craft knife.

3 Work out the positioning and frequency of the stencil along the edges of the cloth and mark lightly with a pencil. These leaves are 10 cm (4 in) apart and 5 cm (2 in) from the edge of the cloth.

4 Water down the fabric paint to the required consistency – about three parts paint to one part water. This 'fuzzes' the edges of the design. Place the stencil over the marked position of the first leaf and apply the paint with a stencil brush.

Move along the tablecloth until your pattern is complete. Leave to dry.

5 Cover the stencilling with a cloth to protect it and iron, using the hottest setting. Then, with a black fabric pen, carefully draw in the veins on each leaf by hand.

6 To make the napkins, cut four 50 cm sq (20 in) pieces and stencil as the tablecloth but along one edge only. Turn under a small hem and sew in place.

The Border

1 Cut four 15 cm (6 in) green strips, one for each side of the cloth. You may need to join the strips to make longer pieces, depending on the size of your tablecloth. Fold them in half lengthways, wrong sides together, and press. Then turn under two 2 cm (¾ in) hems on to the wrong side and press.

3 To make the corners, on the remaining two borders, turn them right sides together and stitch close to the short edges. Turn right sides out and pin to the cloth, and stitch in place.

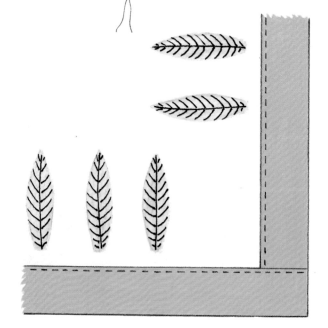

2 Pin a border to two opposite sides of the tablecloth and sew in place.

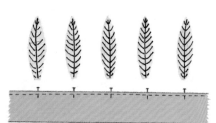

Variation

An alternative to stencilling is to use shop-bought rubber stamps, as above. Or you can cut a simple shape from a sponge. Draw a freehand design on to a car sponge with a felt pen, snip away at the outside edge of the shape with scissors. Your shape should be left in relief and the rest of the sponge cut away. Dip the sponge in the fabric paint, dab off the excess paint and sponge away.

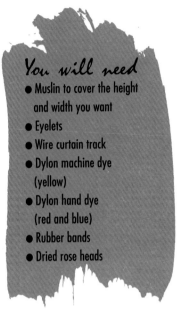

You will need

- Muslin to cover the height and width you want
- Eyelets
- Wire curtain track
- Dylon machine dye (yellow)
- Dylon hand dye (red and blue)
- Rubber bands
- Dried rose heads

Project eight

Muslin curtains with eyelet heading and dried rose heads

If your dining area is part of another room, a muslin curtain can isolate it and create an intimate feel. With this wire-and-eyelet heading it can stretch from wall to wall where there is no other means of support.

1 Measure the drop and width of the curtains. Most muslin comes in 90 cm (36 in) widths, so you will need to sew several widths together.

2 Following the manufacturer's instructions, dye all the muslin yellow with a machine dye in the washing machine. Leave to dry.

3 Cut the muslin to the required drop, and lie the cut lengths on top of each other. They must be dyed together to get the same line when they are sewn together.

4 Mix up the red hand dye in a bucket, following the manufacturer's instructions. Dip the bottom third of all the muslin pieces into the red dye and leave for the required length of time (put the top half of the muslin in a plastic bag to prevent splashing). Hang on the line to dry.

5 Mix up a small amount of blue hand dye. Gather a handful of fabric about 30 cm (12 in) from the bottom of each piece of muslin, where it has been dyed red, and tie a rubber band around each piece. This will give you a tie-dye effect.

6 Dip the muslin in the blue dye and leave for the required amount of time. Drip dry and take the rubber bands out when dry.

7 Sew together two lengths of muslin to make one curtain. Turn over a 3 cm (1¼ in) hem at the top and a 1 cm (½ in) hem at the bottom of the curtain.

8 Work out the position of the eyelets, about every 15 cm (6 in). Position the two sides of the eyelet on either side of the muslin. Hit the top piece with a hammer so that it cuts through the fabric and snaps together with the bottom piece. Place the eyelets on a stable surface when you hit them. It is best to have a practice run first.

9 Repeat the eyelet heading on the other curtain.

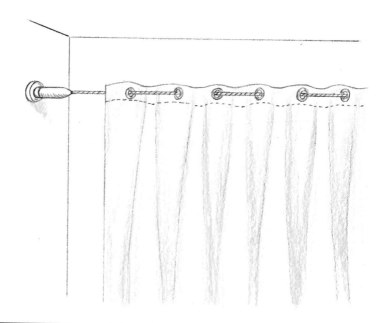

10 Fit the wire track to one wall. Thread the curtains on to the wire and fix the wire track to the opposite wall and pull tight.

11 Sew or pin the dried rose heads on to the yellow part of the curtains.

Variation

This idea will work just as well with a curtain pole attached to the ceiling. Make sure you find the joists to screw into. You could leave the finials off the curtain pole so that the curtain hangs as close to the wall as possible. Leave out the eyelet heading and instead use curtain clips to hook on to the curtain rings.

Project nine
Doing up a junk table and chairs

When you move into a new home, relatives are keen to give you all the things they don't want but are too good to throw out! If you are short of cash – and most of us are – transform their mismatched offerings with a lick of paint and a few sheets of wrapping paper, pictures from magazines or blown-up photocopies. Don't be frightened to give it a go – after all, it won't cost you more than the price of a tin of paint, and even that could be left over from painting the walls!

You will need
- Emulsion paint in four colours
- Fine grade sandpaper
- Wrapping paper
- Acrylic varnish
- Table and chairs
- Spray mount
- Fixative (from art shops) or hairspray

1 The chairs I used were coated in several layers of white gloss paint, so to avoid hours of laborious rubbing down I had them dipped. You can use a paint stripper if there is not too much paint. The table was just sanded lightly with fine-grade sandpaper.

2 Give the chairs and table two coats of lilac-blue emulsion and allow to dry between coats.

3 Apply two coats of soft-green vinyl matt emulsion on top of the blue and allow to dry between coats.

4 Lightly rub away at the edges of the table and chairs with fine-grade sandpaper until the blue shows through. The idea is to make the furniture look as if it has worn naturally.

5 For the découpage, work out how many pictures will fit comfortably on the table and on the backs of the chairs. I used wrapping paper fruit images cut out with a pair of fine-pointed scissors. Spray the front of each image with fixative or hairspray to stop the inks bleeding when they are varnished.

6 Spray the backs of the images with spray mount and arrange around the circumference of the table and on the backs of the chairs. Spray mount allows you to reposition, so it doesn't matter if you don't get it right straight away.

7 Finally, give the table and chairs two or three coats of matt acrylic varnish.

Chair seats

1 These chair seats are the push-out type covered in vinyl.

2 Wash the seats with washing-up liquid and a scrubbing brush to get rid of the years of dirt.

3 Give each seat two or three coats of emulsion. I used orange and mauve to contrast with the green of the rest of the furniture.

4 Apply two or three coats of acrylic matt varnish.

Variation

Instead of wrapping paper, cut out pictures from magazines or blow up lettering on a photocopier. Cut them out and stick them around the circumference of the table and on the backs of the chairs, as with the wrapping paper.
You could use words, such as the names of the people who will sit there or different mealtimes such as breakfast, lunch, tea and supper, maybe in various languages.

Project ten

Swedish-style plate rack

It is a pity to keep pretty plates unseen in a cupboard. This Swedish-style plate rack keeps them on show and at hand for when you need them.

You will need

- 6 mm-thick (¼ in) plywood
- 25 x 100 mm (1 x 4 in) softwood
- 25 x 50 mm (1 x 2 in) softwood
- 18 mm (¾ in) dowel
- PVA glue
- Wood screws
- Panel pins
- Spirit level

1 Cut the plywood to the overall size of the plate rack, in this case 140 x 80 cm (55 x 31½ in). (Check the size of the plates you plan to put into the rack first.) Cut a length of 25 x 100 mm (1 x 4 in) softwood to 140 cm (55 in) and screw and glue to the front bottom edge of the plywood to make the bottom shelf.

2 Cut three 80-cm (31½-in) lengths of 25 x 100 mm (1 x 4 in) to make the uprights that hold the dowels. On one, mark the position of the dowels, about 3 cm (1¼ in) in from the outside edge. Place all three pieces on top of each other and drill the two 1.8 cm (¾ in) holes through all three, to ensure that all the holes are in the same place.

3 Panel pin and glue the supports on to the plywood back and then screw to the bottom shelf from underneath.

4 To make the ledges for the plates to sit on, cut six pieces of 25 x 50 mm (1 x 2 in) softwood to fit between the vertical supports. Mark the lengths of the ledges by measuring them against the inside of the frame.

5 Leaving enough space to put small jugs underneath, mark the position of the first and second ledges with a pencil. Measure up from bottom shelf to ensure that the shelf and ledges are parallel.

6 Drill through the plywood, between the two horizontal lines marking the place of the ledges. Put the ledges in position

and puncture them with a bradawl, through the holes you have just drilled, from the reverse side of the plywood back. Screw into position.

7 Mark the two lengths of the dowel against the frame.

8 Push the dowels through the holes and glue before positioning. Tap through with a hammer against a small block of wood.

9 Fill all the holes with wood filler. Paint and varnish.

10 To fix to the wall, drill through the plywood to the wall with screws close to the four corners and on either side of the centre vertical, top and bottom.

Plate rack cross section

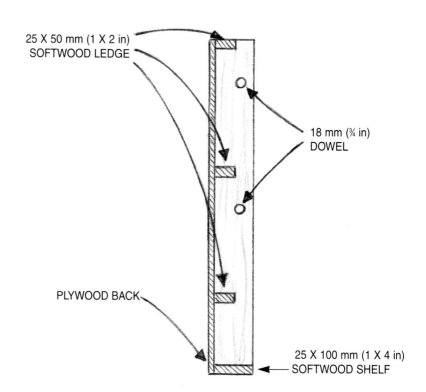

25 X 50 mm (1 X 2 in) SOFTWOOD LEDGE

18 mm (¾ in) DOWEL

PLYWOOD BACK

25 X 100 mm (1 X 4 in) SOFTWOOD SHELF

Plate rack dimensions

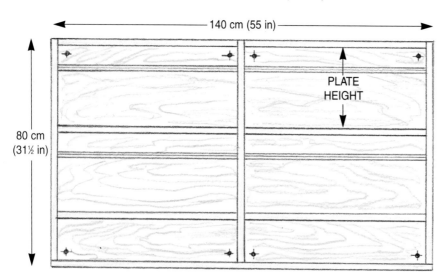

140 cm (55 in)

80 cm (31½ in)

PLATE HEIGHT

Suppliers

CATH KIDSTON
8 Clarendon Cross
London W11 4AP
Tel. 0171 221 4000
page 37 — blue vase
page 29 — tablecloth

CRUCIAL TRADING
Craven Arms
Shropshire SY7 9NY
Tel. 01588 673666
page 57 — seagrass flooring

DALER-ROWNEY
PO Box 10
Bracknell
Berkshire RG12 8ST
Tel. 01344 424621
page 45 — pearlescent paints

DARTINGTON CRYSTAL
Torrington
Devon EX38 7AN
Tel. 01805 622321
page 10 — wine glasses

DULUX
Wexham Road
Slough
Berks SL2 5DS
Tel. 01753 550555
pages 37, 45, 57 & 61 — wall paint

DYLON
Worsley Bridge Road
London SE26 5HD
Tel. 0181 663 4801
pages 49, 51 & 52 — fabric paint and pen
page 55 — machine and cold dye

FABLON ®
Cramlington New Town
Northumberland NE23 8AQ
Tel. 01670 718300
page 44 — sticky-back plastic

McCLOUD & Co
269 Wandsworth Bridge Road
London SW6 2TX
Tel. 0171 371 7151
page 55 — wrought-iron chair

NAIRN CUSHIONFLOR ®
PO BOX 1
Kircaldy
Fife KY1 2SB
Tel. 0345 023166
page 55 — vinyl floor

NICE IRMA'S
46 Goodge Street
London W1P 1FJ
Tel. 0171 580 6921
page 55 — cushions

THE PIER
200 Tottenham Court Road
London W1P 0AD
Tel. 0171 351 7100
page 55 — paper blind

PURVES & PURVES
81 & 83 Tottenham Court Road
London W1P 9HD
Tel. 0171 580 8223
page 37 — Phoenix chairs & white vase
page 55 — red vase

SANDERSON
112-120 Brompton Road
London SW3 1JJ
Tel. 0171 584 3344
pages 31 & 37 — fabric

SPEEDY PRODUCTS
Cheltenham Street
Pendleton
Salford M6 6WY
Tel. 0161 737 1001
page 55 — eyelet heading kit

STANLEY ACMETRACK
Garland Road
East Grinstead
West Sussex RH19 1DR
Tel. 01342 410955
page 47 — sliding door mechanism

Index